Samsung Galaxy User manual For Beginners Seniors

A comprehensive User Guide For Beginners and Seniors to explore the multifaceted capabilities of the Samsung Galaxy A05 and A05S Device like a pro.

Precious Livestone

Table of Contents

11

INTRODUCTION

Discover the interactive and informative User Guide for the Samsung Galaxy A05 and A05S Device, a resource meticulously crafted to enhance your device experience. Regardless of your level of expertise in mobile technology, this essential tool empowers you with the necessary knowledge and skills to effortlessly navigate your device. Immerse yourself in this all-encompassing guide to unlock the full potential of the Samsung Galaxy A05 and A05S Device, unveiling a wealth of invaluable insights and techniques.

Chapter 1
Charging your battery

Ensure that your battery is charged before you use it for the very first time, you can also charge your battery if you know it has not been used for a long period of time.

Only use Samsung-approved battery, cable specially made for your gadget, and charger. Incompatible chargers, batteries, and even cables have the potential to seriously harm you or your device.

- When you connect your charger inappropriately to your device, it can result to serious harm to your device. The warranty does not cover any damage brought on by misuse.

- Only use the USB Type-C cables that came with your device. When you use a Micro USB cord, your device can get damaged.

When your charger isn't in use, unplug it to conserve energy. Since there is no power switch on the charger, you must unplug it from the electrical outlet whenever it is not in usage to prevent power wastage. When charging, your charger must remain near the electrical outlet and be easy to reach as you charge.

Wired charging

To charge battery in your device, insert your USB cable into the multipurpose jack and connect it to your USB power adapter. Once the smartphone has finished charging, unplug your charger from it.

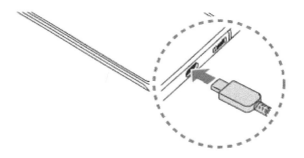

Quick charging your device

Open your Settings application, select Battery & device care → then select Battery → tap on More battery's setting, then you enable your desired feature.

Open the Settings app, press the Battery and device care → Battery → More battery settings, and then enable the feature you like.

- Fast charge: In order to utilize your fast charging capability. You should use any battery charger which support the Adaptive fast charging.

When your device or its screen is off, your battery can be charged even more quicker.

Reducing the consumption of your battery

There are several of options on your device that might help you save your battery life.

- Make use of your device care feature to maximize your device.

- Press your side key to turn off your screen while you're not using your device.

- Switch on the power-savings mode.

- Close down any unused applications.

- Turn off your Bluetooth features when it's not being use.

- Turn off auto-syncing for applications which require to be in sync.

- Decrease the duration of your backlight.

- Reduce the brightness of your screen.

Battery charging advices & precautions

- When your battery is fully drained, your device can't be powered on right away once your charger has been connected. Before using your device, give a discharged battery a few minutes to charge.

- Your battery will run out rapidly if you use network applications, apps that require connectivity to a different device, or multiple applications open at once. Use these applications only when your battery has fully charged to prevent power lost during data transfers.

- When you're using a source of power other than your charger, like a computer, the charging speed may be slower because there is less electrical current.

- While charging, your device could be used; however, the battery could require longer time for it to charge completely.

- Your touchscreen might not work if your device is charging with an irregular power source. Unplug your charger from your device once this happens.

- The smartphone and charger may get heated throughout the charging process. This is typical and shouldn't have an impact on the functionality or lifespan of your device. The charger can stop charging whenever your battery becomes hotter than normal.

- The device might be harmed if it is charged with the multipurpose jack wet.

Before charging your smartphone, make sure the multipurpose jack is completely dry.

- Take your device and charger to an authorized Samsung service center if the charging isn't working properly.

Chapter 2
SIM / USIM (nano-SIM cards) card

Insert your SIM or the USIM card that the mobile service provider has given you.

If you want two distinct phone numbers / service providers on just one device, you can enter 2 SIM or the USIM cards. In certain regions, inserting two different SIM cards into a device may result in slower data transfer rates than inserting a single SIM card.

Depending on your provider, certain services that need a network connectivity might be unavailable.

Installing your SIM / USIM card

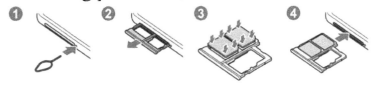

1   Insert your ejection pin to the opening adjacent to it to release your tray.

2   Gently remove your tray from its try slot.

3   Position your SIM / USIM card in your tray having your gold-coloured contacts placed facing

down and carefully press your SIM / USIM card to your tray to safeguarded it.

4   Reposition the tray within your tray slot.

- Only use nano-SIM cards.

- Take care not to misplace or allow unauthorized use of your SIM / USIM card. Any losses or inconveniences brought on by misplaced and stolen cards are not Samsung's responsibility.

- Verify that there is a perpendicular ejection pin to the hole. If not, your device can become damaged

- Your SIM card could come loose or fall out from the tray if it is not firmly inserted.

- Your device can get damaged if you put your tray into it when it's wet. Ensure that your tray is always dry.

- To avoid liquid from getting inside your device, make sure the tray is fully inserted into your tray slot.

SIM cards manager

Open your Settings application, then you tap on Connections → select SIM cards manager.

- SIMs cards: You should Activate your SIM card for use as well as personalize the settings of your SIM card.

- Preferred SIM cards: You can choose which of your SIM to use for certain features, like voice calls, whenever two of your SIM cards are active.

- Automatic data switching's: If your device's chosen SIM card is unable to establish a network connection, configure it to use a different SIM card as your data service.

- More SIM cards settings: Tailor calls settings to your preferences.

Your memory card (the microSD cards)

Installing your memory card

The memory card's capacity of your device, may differ from different models, and depending on the manufacturer & type of memory card, certain memory cards might not work on your device. To see your maximum memory card's capacity for your device, check it out on the Samsung web page.

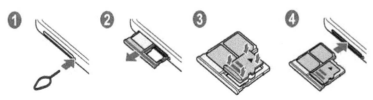

1   Insert your ejection pin to the opening adjacent to it to release your tray.

2   Gently remove your tray from its try slot.

3   Position your SIM / USIM card in your tray having your gold-coloured contacts placed facing down and carefully press your SIM / USIM card to your tray to safeguarded it.

4   Reposition the tray within your tray slot.

• Your device might not be completely compatible with all memory cards. Using any incompatible card could corrupt your data saved on your memory card or harm the device itself.

• Carefully insert your memory card so that is right-side up.

- Verify that there is a perpendicular ejection pin to the opening. If not, there could be damage to your device.

- Your mobile network connection is going to be turned off whenever you remove your tray from your smartphone.

- Your memory card could come loose or fall off from the tray if it is not firmly inserted.

- Your device can get damaged if you put your tray into it when it's wet. Ensure that your tray is always dry.

- Place your tray into your tray slot all the way, to avoid liquid from getting into your device.

- For your memory cards, the device is compatible with both the FAT & exFAT files systems. Your device will either request that you reformat your card when you insert one that was formatted from another file system or it won't recognize it at all. You must format your memory card before using it. Speak with a Samsung Service Center or your memory card manufacturer when your device is having trouble formatting or recognizing the card.

- Your Memory cards lose life if data is whitethorn and erased frequently.

- Whenever you are inserting memory card to your device, your memory card's file folder appears on the My Files → then SD card's folder.

Removing your memory card
Prior to removing your memory card, you should first dismount it for safer removal.

1   Open your Settings application, then tap on Battery & devices care → select Storage.

2   For viewing the page of your SD card wipe towards your left.

3   Then Tap on ⋮ → Unmount.

Never take out external storage, like a memory card or USB drive, while your device is accessing or transmitting data, or immediately thereafter. By doing this, you run the risk of corrupting or losing data as well as damaging your external storage /

device. Any damages, including lost data, brought on by improper usage of your external storage gadgets are not Samsung's responsibility.

Formatting your memory card

Your device might not be able to use memory card that has been formatted using a computer. Format your memory card in your device.

1	Open your Settings app, then tap on Battery & devices care → then select Storage.

2	For viewing the page of your SD card swipe towards the left.

3	Then tap on ⋮ → Format.

Don't forget to create backup copies for every of your important information kept on your memory card before formatting it. Data loss arising from user actions is not covered by your manufacturer's warranty.

Chapter 3
Turning on & off your device

Adhere to every posted warnings & instructions from authorized officials in locations where the usage of wireless gadgets is prohibited, like hospitals and airplanes.

Turning on your device
To power on your device, briefly press & hold your Side key.

Turning off your device
1   For turning your device off, you should press & hold-down your Side key. You can additionally, open your notification panel, then you swipe down, and then you tap ⏻.

2   Then tap on Power off.

In order to restart your device, you should tap on Restart.

Force restart

To restart your smartphone if it's frozen or its unresponsive, you should press & hold down your Side & Volume Down keys at the same time for longer than seven seconds.

Emergency mode

To save battery life, you can put your device in emergency mode. There will be restrictions on some apps and features. You may place an emergency call, notify people of your present location, play an emergency alarm, & much more when you are in an emergency mode. For activation of emergency mode, you should press & hold down your side key, then you tap on Emergency mode. As an alternative, swipe downward to reveal your notification panel, then tap on ⏻ → Emergency mode.

For disabling your emergency mode, you should tap on ⋮ → then Turns off Emergency modes.

The remaining time before your battery runs out is indicated by your usage that time left. Based on the settings of your device and operating circumstances, the remaining usage time might vary.

Initial setup

Comply with your on-screen steps for setting up your mobile device after you turn it on for the very first times or after executing data reset.

In your initial setup process, you might be unable to configure certain device features if you are not connected to a WiFi connection.

Fingerprint recognition

For your fingerprint recognition to work, you have to register the information of your fingerprint and sav it on your device.

- The availability of this feature could vary based on the model or service provider.

- Fingerprint recognition increases device security by utilizing the distinctive qualities of each of your fingerprint. There is virtually little chance that your fingerprint sensor will confuse two distinct fingerprints. Nonetheless, the sensor might identify two fingerprints as same in rare instances when they are strikingly similar.

- Verify that the screen protector you use let you to use your on-screen fingerprint's sensor.

- When you employ your fingerprint for screen lock, you won't be able to use it to unlock your screen first time your device is turned on. You have to enter your PIN, password or pattern you selected when registering your fingerprint to unlock your screen in order to use the device. Ensure that you don't forget your PIN, password, pattern.

- Whenever your fingerprint fails to be recognized, unlock your device with your PIN, password, pattern, that you set while you were registering your fingerprint e-register your fingerprints. You aren't going to be able to utilize your device when you fail to reset it in the event that you forget your PIN, pattern, or password. Any loss of data or trouble brought on by misplaced unlock codes is not Samsung's fault.

- Each of your biometrics' information will be erased if you use the less secure screen lock methods of Swipe or None. You must reregister your biometric information if you wish to utilize it in apps or other services.

For improved fingerprints recognition

The following factors could impact the functionality of this feature if you scanned your finger prints on your device:

- If your fingerprints are wrinkled or have scars, your device might be unable to recognize it.

- Fingerprints from tiny or small fingers, may not be recognizable by your device.

- In order to enhance recognition performance, register the fingerprints of your hand that is most frequently used to operate your device.

- Your device possesses an integrated recognition fingerprint sensor on the centre of the bottom of your screen. Make sure that no objects, including keys, coins, pens, or necklaces, are scratching or damaging your fingerprint's recognition sensor part of your touchscreen or your screen protector.

- Make sure your fingers are dry and clean, as well as your fingerprint's recognition sensors area located in the bottom center of your screen.

- Your device might not recognize your fingerprint's if you use your fingertips or bend your finger. Press on your screen until your fingertip covers the entire area of your fingerprint recognition. To improve recognition performance, please register your fingerprints with the hand that you used mostly to achieve tasks on the device.

Registering your fingerprints on your device

1	Open your Settings application then you tap on Biometrics & security → then select Fingerprints.

2	Then read Your on-screen directions then tap on Continue.

3	Then you select and set any screen lock style.

4   Put your finger up against your sensor for fingerprint recognition. Raise your finger and reposition it on your fingerprint recognition sensor if your device has detected it.

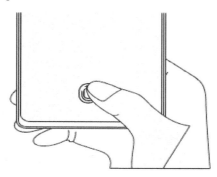

Continue doing this until your fingerprint is completely registered.

5   Press Done once you've completed registering your finger prints. selecting Checks added fingerprints, you may see if your fingerprint has been registered.

Unlocking your screen using your fingerprints

Using your fingerprint, rather than a PIN, pattern, or password, you may unlock your screen.

1 Open your Settings app then tap on Biometrics & security → then select Fingerprints.

2 Then unlock your screen with your preset screen's lock style.

3   Then tap on Fingerprint unlocks switch for activating it.

4   On your locked screen, you should put your finger in the recognition sensor of your fingerprint then you scan fingerprint.

Changing the icon setting of your fingerprint

If you tap your screen while your screen is off, you can configure your device to display or hide your fingerprint's recognition icon.

1 Open your Settings application and tap Biometrics and security → Fingerprints.

2 Then Unlock your screen with your preset method of screen lock.

3 Then tap on Shows icon when screen is off then you choose an option.

Deleting your registered fingerprints

Your registered fingerprints can be deleted.

1 Open your Settings application then tap on Biometrics & security → then tap Fingerprints.

2 Then unlock your screen with your preset method of screen lock.

3 After which choose any fingerprint for deletion then you tap on Remove.

Face recognition

Your device may set to unlock your screen by your facial recognition.

- The very first time you unlock your screen after turning on your device, you will not be able to utilize your face for a screen lock system. You have to enter your PIN, pattern, or password that selected when registering your face to unlock your screen in order to use your device. Take cautious not to lose the details of your password, PIN, or pattern.

- Every last one of your biometric's information will be erased if you choose the less secure screen lock options of swipe / None. You must reregister your biometric information if you wish to utilize it in apps or other services.

Precautions when employing your face recognition

Take note of these precautions prior to using your device's face recognition feature.

- Your device might be unlocked through something or somebody which resembles your image.
- Your face recognition remains less secure compared to Pattern, Password, or PIN.

To improve face recognition
Put in mind these below when employing your face recognition:

- When registering, take into account these conditions, like wearing, hats, glasses, masks, heavy makeup or beards.
- Make sure your camera's lens is clean and that you in an adequately lit area.
- Make sure your image appears sharp for more accurate results.

Register your face
Register your entire face indoors & away from sunlight for optimal face registration.

1   Open your Settings application then tap Biometrics & security → select Face recognition.

2   Then read your on-screen's instructions then tap on Continue.

3   Then you set any method of screen lock.

4   You should then place your face within your frame of your screen. Then your camera will get your face scanned.

- In the event that using your face to unlock your device screen isn't functioning properly, you can re-register your face by removing it by tapping Removes faces data.

- To improve facial recognition, select Add Alternative appearances to enhance recognition then you add an alternative appearance.

Unlocking your screen using face

You may unlock your screen using your face rather than using a password., pattern, or PIN.

1 Open your Settings app then tap on Biometrics & security → select Face recognition.

2 Then unlock your screen with your preset lock screen method.

3 Then tap your Face unlocks switch for activating it.

4 Then your locked screen, look at on screen.

You don't need to use any other screen lock methods once your face has been recognized. Use your preset lock-screen method when your face does not appear to be recognized.

Deleting your registered facial data

You may decide the to delete your registered face data.

1 Open your Settings app then tap on Biometrics & security → select Face recognition.

2 Then unlock your screen with your preset lock screen method.

3 Then you tap on Remove faces data → then tap on Remove.

Once your registered face gets deleted, every related feature is going to be deactivated also.

Chapter 4
Camera

Introduction

You can capture your pictures & your record videos by employing different modes & settings.

The Camera etiquette

- Do not capture pictures or record videos of someone else without their consent;

- Don't capture pictures or videos in areas where it is against the law

- Don't take pictures or videos in locations where you might infringe upon the privacy of others.

Capturing your photos

1 Open your Camera application.

Alternatively, you can drag your app to the left side on your locked screen or quickly pressing your side key twice to open it.

- while you open your Camera application from your locked screen or while your screen is off when your screen lock's method is enabled, certain camera features will not be accessible.

- When not in use, your camera turns off automatically.

Certain methods might not be accessible based on your model or service provider.

2 Wherever your camera is supposed to focus, tap your image on your preview screen.

You should drag on your adjustment bar which displays above or beneath your circular frame to change your brightness of the image.

3. To take a picture, tap ⭕ .

To switch your shooting mode, wipe right or left on your preview screen, or drag on your shooting mode menu toward your right or left.

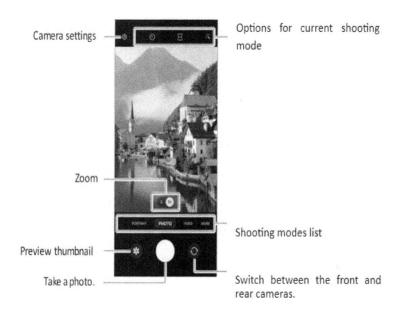

Camera settings

Options for current shooting mode

Zoom

Preview thumbnail

Take a photo.

Shooting modes list

Switch between the front and rear cameras.

- Depending upon the camera being used and your shooting mode, a vary preview screens might show up.

- Whenever capturing photos or videos using high resolution / higher-zoom ratio, your focus might not be clear when your subject become close. Capture images or videos at a reasonable distance away.

- Try cleaning your camera's lens & taking another shot if your photos come out blurry.

- Verify that there are no contaminants or damage to your lens. If not, your device might not function correctly in certain modes that need high resolutions.

- The camera on your device features lens that is wide-angle. Wide-angle images or videos may contain slight distortion, which is not a sign of your device performance issue.

- Depending on your resolution, a video's maximum recording capacity could vary.

- Your camera may form condensation or fog up when your device gets exposed to a sudden change in the air temperature, as a result of the temperature differences between the inside and outside camera cover. Ensure to avoid conditions such as this when you intend to use your camera. If fogging doesn't happen, should allow your camera to naturally dry at room temperature prior to shooting pictures or recording videos, if not your outcome might appear blurry.

Using your camera button

- For recording your video, press & hold down your camera button.

- for burst shots, you should swipe your camera button towards the edge of your screen & hold it.

- You may take more convenient pictures by moving your camera button around on your screen by adding another one. In your preview screen, you should tap on ⚙ → Shooting methods then you tap your Floating Shutter's button toggle for activating it.

Photo mode

To make taking pictures easier, your camera automatically modifies your shooting settings based on your surroundings.

On your shooting modes lists, then tap on PHOTO then you tap ○ to capture a photo.

Capturing your selfies

Take self-portraits with your front camera.

1 On your preview screen, you should swipe up or down, or you tap on ⊚ for switching to your front camera to take a self-portrait.

2 Then face the lens of your front camera.

For taking your self-portraits using a wide-angled shot for people or landscape, tap 👥 on.

3 Then tap on ◯ to take your photo.

Applying filters & beauty effects

Before taking your picture, you can choose any filter effect & adjust your facial attributes like the tone of your skin or the shape of your face.

1   On your preview screen, you should tap ☀

2   Choose any effects then take your photo.

Locking your focus (AF) & exposure (AE)

To stop your camera from adjusting automatically due to changes to your subjects or the source of your light, you may lock your focus or your exposure to a specified area.

When you tap & hold down on the focus area, your focus & exposure settings become locked in and your

AF/AE frames will display in the area. The lock is maintained regardless of when you take your picture.

Video mode

To make recording videos easier, your camera adjusts its shooting options based on its surroundings.

1   On your shooting modes menu, tap on VIDEO then you tap on ⬤ to record your video.

- Tap ⬤ to snap an image from the video when you are performing recording.

- Press and hold where you wish to focus, to change the focus when you are shooting a video. To use the auto focus mode, you can tap on 🔒 to cancel the manually set focus.

2   Tap on ⬤ stop recording your video.

Portrait mode

With your camera, you may capture pictures where your subject is the main focus standing out so clearly and your background is blurry.

1 On your shooting modes menu, tap on PORTRAIT.

2 Then drag the adjustment bar of your background blur for adjusting the level of blur.

3 Once Ready displays on your preview screen, then tap on ◯ to take your photo.

Background blur adjustment bar

- Make use of this feature at an area with sufficient lighting.
- In these kinds of circumstances, your background blur might not be applied correctly:

✓ When your device or your subject is constantly moving.

✓ When your subject is very thin or even transparent.

✓ When your subject possesses an identical colour to that if your background.

✓ When your subject or the background is quite plain.

Pro mode

The Pro mode helps you capture pictures while manually modifying your different shooting options, like your exposure and ISO values.

Tap on MORE → then select PRO from your menu of shooting modes. To snap a picture, choose an option, then adjust your settings, then you tap on ⬤ .

Available options

- ISO: Choose any ISO value. It manages the light sensitivity of your camera. Low values apply to objects that are still or well-lit. Higher values apply to objects that move quickly or have poor lighting. Greater ISO settings, however, may cause noise in your photos.

- EV: Modify your exposure value. This sets the amount of light that reaches your camera's sensor. To compensate for poor light, increase your exposure.

- WB: Choose a suitable white balance to ensure that photos have a realistic color spectrum. Your color temperature is adjustable.

Separating your focus area & your area of exposure

Your focus area & your exposure area can be separated. Touch and hold your preview screen. Your screen will display your AF/AE frame. To divide your focus area from your exposure area, you should drag on your frame to your spot you want.

Panorama mode

The panorama mode can be use, to take multiple photos then stitches all of them together in order to create wide scene.

1 In your shooting modes menu, tap on MORE → then select PANORAMA.

2 Then tap on ◯ then move your device slowly towards one direction.

Retain your image in your viewfinder of your camera. Your device will stop taking pictures automatically when your preview image stands outside of the guiding frame or if you refrain from moving your device.

3 Then tap on ⬤ to cease taking photos.

You should avoid capturing pictures having backgrounds which are indistinct, such as a plain wall or empty sky.

Food mode

Capture pictures of food having more vivid colours.

1 On your shooting modes menu, tap MORE → FOOD.

2 Tap your screen then drag on that circular frame across the area for highlighting.

Area outside your circular frame gets blurred.

For resizing your circular frame, you should drag any corner of your frame.

3 Then tap ᐁ & drag your adjustment bar for adjusting your colour tone.

4 Tap on ◯ to take your photo.

Customizing the settings of your camera

On your preview screen, you should tap on ⚙. Certain options might be unavailable based on your shooting mode.

Intelligent features

- Scene optimizer: Configure your device to automatically apply an optimal effect based on your subject / scene and adjust your color settings.

- Scans QR code: From your preview screen, configure your device for scanning QR codes.

Pictures

- Swipe the shutter's button to: Choose any action to execute once you swipe your camera button towards the edge of your screen & hold it.

- Highs-efficiency pictures: Use the High Efficiencies Images Format (The HEIF) when taking images.

Selfies

- Saves selfies as preview: Configure your device to save front-facing camera photographs exactly as they display on your preview screen, without cropping or rotating them.

Videos

- Reduced files sizes: Videos using the format of High Efficiency Video's Codec (HEVC) can be recorded. To preserve the memory of your device, your HEVC videos should be saved in compressed files.

The HEVC videos cannot be shared online or played on any other device.

General

- Auto HDR: Capture your images with vibrant colors and accurately capture details in both bright & dark conditions.
- Grid lines: Show viewfinder guidelines to aid in subject selection and composition.

- Locations tags: Allows you attach your GPS location's tag to your photo.

- The strength of your GPS signal could decrease within locations in which your signal gets blocked, like between the buildings or in areas with low elevation, or during adverse weather conditions.

- If you upload your images online, they can show up having your location on them. Turn off your location tag settings to prevent this.

- Shooting methods: Choose several shooting methods to capture images or videos.

- Settings to keeps: When you first open your camera, save your last settings that you used, like your shooting mode.

- Storage location: Choose the memory-based storage location. Inserting a memory card will trigger the appearance of this feature.

- Watermark: When shooting photos, place a watermark on your lower left corner of your picture.

Privacy

- Privacy Notice: Click here to view your privacy notice.

- Permissions: Check out the permissions needed for using your Camera app.

- Reset: Reset your camera's settings.

- About the Camera: Check your legal information & version of your Camera application.

- Contact us: See frequently asked question or ask questions View the privacy notice.

Certain features might not be accessible based on your model.

Samsung account

Your Samsung's account serves as an incorporated account service which enables you to make use of several kinds of Samsung service offered on smartphones, TVs, & Samsung website. Go to account.samsung.com to view list of the services which are supported with your Samsung account.

1 Open your Settings application then tap on Samsung accounts.

Alternatively, you can Open your Settings app then tap on Accounts & backup → then select Manage accounts → the Add account → then tap on Samsung account.

2 when you already own a Samsung's account, you should sign into your Samsung's account.

- When you desire to log in via your Google's account, you should tap on Continue with Google's.

- When you don't own any Samsung's account, you should tap on Create account.

Finding ID & resetting password

On your Samsung account's sign-in screens, select Find ID / Forgot password? if you can't remember your ID of the Samsung account or its password. Once you've entered the necessary information, you can retrieve your ID or change your password.

Signing out from Samsung account

Your data, including contacts and events, will be erased from your mobile device once you log out of your Samsung's account.

1   Open your Settings app then you tap on Accounts & backup →then select Manage accounts.

2   Then tap on Samsung account → then select My profile then you tap on Sign out on the bottom screen.

3   Then tap on the Sign out, type in your password of the Samsung account, then you tap on OK.

Chapter 5
Understanding your screen
Controlling your touchscreen

Tapping

Tap the screen.

Tapping and holding

Tap and hold the screen for approximately 2 seconds.

Dragging

Tap and hold an item and drag it to the target position.

Double-tapping

Double-tap the screen.

Swiping

Swipe upwards, downwards, to the left, or to the right.

Spreading and pinching

Spread two fingers apart or pinch on the screen.

- Avoid letting your touchscreen make contact with any other electrical equipment. Problems regarding your touchscreen may arise from electrostatic discharges.

- Avoid using sharp objects to tap your touchscreen or exerting too much pressure using your fingertips to prevent damage.

- It is advised against using fixed graphics in any portion of your touchscreen for prolonged periods of time. Ghosting or afterimages (screen burn-in) could occur from doing this.

Touch inputs that are made outside of your touch input area, near your screen's edges, might not be recognized by your device.

Navigation bar (the easy buttons)

Your soft button will show up on your bottom navigation bar of your screen once you turn it on. By default, the Recents, Home, and Back buttons are assigned to your soft buttons. Depending on the application being used or the user's situation, your button functionality may vary.

Button		Function
|||	Recents	• Tap to open the list of recent apps.
◯	Home	• Tap to return to the Home screen. • Tap and hold to launch the **Google Assistant** app.
‹	Back	• Tap to return to the previous screen.

Hiding your navigation bar

To utilize apps or view files on a larger screen, hide your navigation bar.

Open your Settings application, then tap on Display → then select Navigation bar, then you tap on Swipe gestures beneath Navigation type. The gesture indications will show up and your navigation bar disappears. Choose an option by tapping More options.

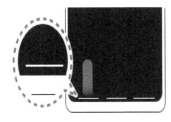

Swipe from bottom   Swipe from sides and bottom

To disable your gesture hint feature and hide it from view, simply tap on the Gesture hint toggle at your bottom screen.

Home screen & Applications screen

All of the features on your device may be accessed from your Home screen. Widgets, application shortcuts, and other information are displayed. The Applications screen shows icons for each of the applications, which includes recently installed applications.

Switch between your Home & Applications screens

Swipe up to reveal your Applications screen from your Home screen.

Swipe up or down on your Applications screen to get back to your Home screen. As an alternative, you can tap your Back or Home buttons.

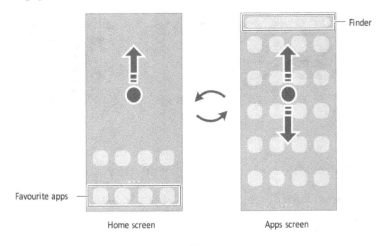

Favourite apps

Finder

Home screen   Apps screen

You may tap your application screen to access it when you add your Apps button to your Home screen. To enable the Show Applications screens button on Home's screen's switch, tap & hold down an empty spot on your Home screen, select Settings, then tap the button. On the bottom of your Home screen, an Applications button gets added.

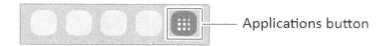 Applications button

Edit your Home screen

To access the editing tools on your Home screen, you should pinch your two fingers together or simply tap & hold down any empty spot. In addition, you may set up widgets and change your wallpaper and many more. Additionally, you can reorganize, delete, or add Home screen's panels.

- Adding up panels: Swipe toward your left, then you tap on ⊕.

- Moving panels: A panel preview can be moved by tapping and holding it, then dragging it to the new spot you want it.

- Remove the panels: tap 🗑on panel.

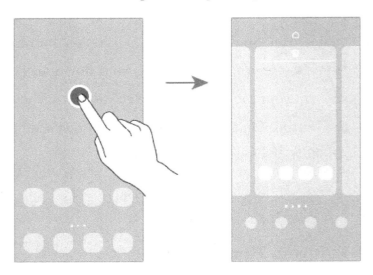

- The wallpaper & style: Customize your locked screen's and your home screen's wallpaper.

- Themes: Modify the theme on your device. Depending on your theme chosen, the interface's visual components—such as colors, icons, & wallpaper—will alter.

- Widgets: On your Home screen, widgets are little applications that initiate particular app functions to offer information and easy access. After choosing a widget, tap on Add. Your Home screen will now have the widget.

- Settings: Adjust the Home screen's configuration, including the screen arrangement.

Displaying all the applications on your Home screen

You can configure your device to display every application on your Home screen, doing away with the need for a separate Applications panel. On your Home screen, you should tap & hold down any empty spot, then tap on Settings → then select Home screens layouts → then tap on Home screens only → then select Apply.

Now, swipe left on your Home screen to access all of your applications.

Launching the Finder

Quickly look for content in your device.

1 On your Applications screen, you should tap on Search. Alternatively, you can open your notification panel, then swipe downwards, after which then tap on

Q.

2 Type in a keyword.

The applications & the content of your device is going to be searched for.

When you tap on Q on your keyboard, it allows you to search for many more contents.

Moving the items

An object can be moved by tapping and holding it, then dragging it to the new spot you want it to be. Drag your item towards any side of your screen to move it to a different panel.

To add shortcut to an application on your Home screen, you should tap & hold down any item on your Apps screen, then you tap on Adds to Home. The app will have a shortcut added to your Home screen. Additionally, you can relocate often used applications to your Home screen's shortcut area on the bottom.

Creating folders

To access and start applications fast, organize comparable apps into folders.

You may move one app over another app by tapping and holding it on your Apps or Home screens.

Your chosen applications will be placed in a brand-new folder. To input the name of a folder, tap on Folder name.

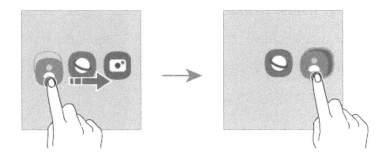

Adding more applications

On your folder, you should tap on ✚. To add applications, choose them, then press Done. An application can also be added simply dragging it into a folder.

Moving applications from folder

Tap & hold an application to drag the application into a new spot.

Deleting folder

After holding down a folder, select Delete folder. The folder alone will get deleted. The applications that are in your folder will move to your Apps screen.

Edge panel

The Edge panels allow you to easily access your favorite applications and features. To enable your Edge panels handle, launch your Settings application, choose Display, then tap your Edge panels switch. Alternatively, you can drag your Edge panel handle to the center of your screen.

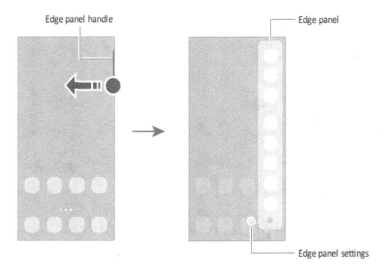

Edge panel handle

Edge panel

Edge panel settings

Lock screen

Your Side key is used to lock & turn off your screen. Additionally, when your device has not been used for a predetermined amount of time, your screen automatically locks & turns off.

When your screen turns on, swipe to any direction to unlock it.

To turn your screen on if it's off, press your Side key. You might also double-tap your screen.

Changing the method of your screen lock

Open your Settings application, choose a method by tapping Lock screen → then tap on Screen lock type, then you change your screen lock's method.

By limiting access to your device, you may protect even your personal info whether you use a PIN, password, pattern, or data of your biometric as a method of screen lock. When your screen lock's method is enabled, your device will always need an unlock code to be unlocked.

If you type your unlock code wrongly multiple times in succession and exceed the number of attempts, you have the option to force a factory reset of your data on your device. To activate your preset screen-locking method, open your Settings app, then select Lock screen → then tap on Secured lock settings, then you unlock your screen, and press your Auto factory's reset toggle.

Indicator icons

On your status bar on your top screen, there are indicator icons. The most popular icons are those found in the below table.

Icon	Meaning
⊘	No signal
⌀ıl	Signal strength
ᴿ⌀ıl	Roaming (outside of normal service area)
G	GPRS network connected
E	EDGE network connected
3G	UMTS network connected
H	HSDPA network connected
H+	HSPA+ network connected
Icon	Meaning
4G / LTE	LTE network connected
5G	5G network connected
5G	LTE network connected in LTE network that includes the 5G network
📶	Wi-Fi connected
∗	Bluetooth feature activated
⦿	Location services being used
📞	Call in progress
⤫	Missed call
▣	New text or multimedia message
⏰	Alarm activated
🔇 / 📳	Mute mode / Vibration mode
✈	Flight mode activated
⚠	Error occurred or caution required
/	Battery charging / Battery power level

- In certain apps, the status bar might not show up at the top of the screen. Drag the status bar down from the top of the screen to see it.

- Certain indicator icons can only be seen when your notification panel is opened.

- The indication icons can appear differently based on your model or service provider.

Entering your text

Layout of keyboard

Your keyboard will automatically appear once you type in text.

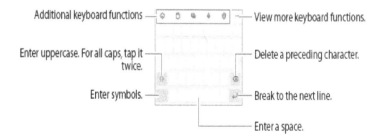

Additional keyboard functions — View more keyboard functions.

Enter uppercase. For all caps, tap it twice. — Delete a preceding character.

Enter symbols. — Break to the next line.

Enter a space.

Some languages do not support text entry. You need to switch your input language to a different one of the supported languages in order to enter in your text.

Changing your input languages

You should tap on ⚙ → then select Languages & types → then tap on Manage inputs languages then choose your language for use. If you choose more than one language, you may switch among your input languages via swiping towards your left / right on your space key.

Changing your keyboard

On your navigation bar, you should tap on ⌨ to change your keyboard.

To change your keyboard type, you should tap on → then select Languages & types, choose any language, then choose your keyboard type that you want.

- Open your Settings app, select General management → then you tap Keyboard list & default, and then tap your Keyboard's button on the navigation's bar switch to enable it if your keyboard button (⌨) is not visible on the bar.

- A key contains between three and four characters in 3 x 4 keyboards. For entering a character, keep tapping your corresponding key until the character you want appears.

Copying & pasting

1   You should tap & hold over any text.

2   Then drag 🔵 or 🔵 you choose your desired text; you can even tap on Select all for selecting all text.

3   Then you can tap on Copy / Cut.

The carefully chosen text is copied to the clipboard.

4To insert your text, press & hold the desired location, then tap Paste.

To insert previously copied text, press Clipboard & choose your text.

Installing / uninstalling applications

Galaxy Store

Download and purchase your applications. Apps developed specifically for the Samsung Galaxy smartphones are available for download.

Open your Galaxy Store application. You can tap on Q to search for new keyword or browse applications by category.

- The availability of this app may vary based on your model or service provider.

- Tap on Menu → ⚙ → then select Auto updates apps, choose an option, and then adjust your auto updates settings.

Play Store

Purchase & download applications.

Open your Play Store application. Apps can be found by keyword search or by browsing by category. Tapping your account icon, choosing Settings → then select Network preferences → then select Auto-updates apps, then choose an option will allow you to change your auto updates settings.

Managing your applications
Uninstalling / disabling applications

You should tap & hold an application then select any option.

- Uninstall: Uninstall downloaded applications.

- Disable: This disables your chosen default applications which cannot uninstalled from your device. Certain applications might not support the feature.

Enabling your applications

Open your Settings app, then tap on Apps → ⬛
→select Disabled → tap on OK, choose any app, then tap on Enable.

Setting up your app permissions

Certain apps may require permission for access to or utilize information from your smartphone in order to function properly.

Open your Settings app, select Apps to see your permissions for apps. After choosing an app, tap on Permissions. Both viewing and changing your app's permissions are possible.

Open your Settings app, then select Apps →⋮→ then tap on Permission manager, then change your app's permission settings by category. Choose an item then choose any application.

Whenever you fail to give permissions to applications, the fundamental features of your applications might not work properly.

Chapter 6
Phone

Introduction

You can make / answer voice & video calls.

Unwanted noises might occur over a call when the area surrounding your upper microphone are covered. Take away accessories, like a stickers or screen protector, surrounding your upper microphone's area.

Making calls

1 Open your Phone app then tap on the Keypad.

2 Enter any phone number.

3 Then tap on 📞 for making a voice call, or 📹 you tap 📷 for making video call.

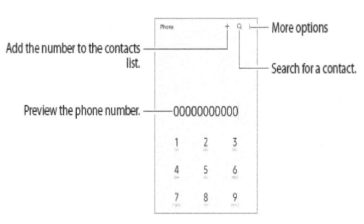

Placing calls from your call logs / contacts list

Open your Phone application, then tap on Recents/Contacts, then swipe towards your right on a phone number or a contact to place a call.

When this feature gets disabled, tap on ⋮ → then select Settings → then tap Other calls settings, then you tap on the Swipes to call / text toggle for activating it.

Using the speed dial

To put a number in speed dial. Open your Phone app, select Keypads or Contacts → ⋮ → then Speed dials numbers, choose any speed dialing number, then add up any phone number. Tap & hold down any speeds dial number in your keypad to place a call. Tap on your first digit / digits of your number, next tap & hold the final digit for speed dialing numbers 10 & up.

For instance, if you've configured 123 for a speed dials number, press 1 and 2 then you tap and hold down 3.

Making international calls

1   Open your Phone app then you tap on Keypad.

2   Then tap & hold 0 till this + is seem sign appears.

75

3   Enter in your country code, phone number, and then tap on 🔵 .

Receiving calls

Answering calls

If you receive a call, you should drag on ⌣ outside your large circle.

Rejecting calls

Drag ⌢ beyond the big circle whenever you receive a call.

When you reject incoming call, you can slide the deliver message bar up and choose your message to be sent.

Open your Phone app, touch ⋮ → then select Settings → then tap on Quick declines messages, type a message, then tap ➕ to create different rejection messages.

Block phone numbers

You can block calls of particular numbers added into your block lists.

76

1   Open your Phone app then tap ⁝→ then select Settings → then tap Block numbers.

2   Then tap on Recents / Contacts, choose phone numbers or contacts, then tap on Done. For manually entering a number, you should tap on Adds phone number, then enter phone number, then you tap ┼.

You won't be notified whenever blocked numbers attempt to reach you. The calls are going to be recorded in your call log.

Incoming calls from individuals who do not display their caller ID can also be blocked. To enable the feature, tap on your Block unknown/private numbers toggle.

Contacts

Introduction

You can manage contacts or create new ones on your mobile device.

Add contacts
Creating new contacts

1 Open your Contacts app then tap ┼.

2 Choose your storage location.

77

3 Then enter the contact information then you tap on Save.

Importing contacts

You can add contacts into your device via importing them via other storage devices.

1   Open your Contacts app then tap $\equiv$ → select Manage contacts → then tap Import / export contacts → then select Import.

2   Follow your on-screen direction for importing contacts.

Synchronizing your contacts with web accounts

Sync the contacts on your device with the contacts online that are saved on your web-based accounts, like the Samsung account.

1   Open your Settings app, then tap Accounts & backup → then select Manage accounts then choose those account for syncing with.

2   After which tap on Sync account then you tap on the Contacts toggle for activating it.

Searching for your contacts

Open your Contacts app. Then tap ^{Q} on the top of your contacts list, then enter the search criteria.

Tap on your contact. Then do any of these actions:

- 📞 : Making voice call.

- 📹 / 📹 : Making video call.

- 💬 : Composing your message.

- ✉️ : Composing an email.

Delete your contacts

1   Open your Contacts app then tap ⋮ → select Delete contacts.

2   Choose contacts then tap on Delete.

For deletion of contact one at a time, select it from your contacts list, then select More → and then tap Delete.

Share your contacts

By using different sharing options, you may share your contacts to other people.

1   Open your Contacts app then tap on $\vdots$ → then select Share contacts.

2   Choose contacts then tap on Share.

3   Choose any sharing method.

Create groups

You may manage contacts via group and add groups, like friends or family.

1   Open your Contacts app then tap ≡ → then select Groups → tap on Create group.

2   Adhere to your on-screen directions for creating a group.

Merging your duplicated contacts

when your list of contacts includes replicate contacts, you should merge these contacts to one to help in streamlining your contacts list.

1   Open your Contacts app then tap on ≡ → then select Manage contacts → then tap Merge contacts.

2   Then tick your contacts then tap Merge.

Messages

Introduction

You can send & receive messages based on conversation.

Sending and receiving messages when roaming may result in additional charges.

Send messages

1 Open your Messages application and tap on 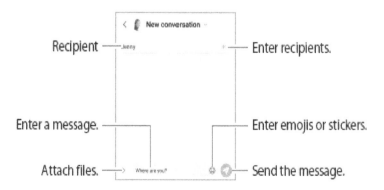.

 2 Add up recipients then enter your message.

For recording and sending voice message, you should

tap & hold ᶦᪧᪧᶦ , say your message, then you release your finger. Only when there is nothing in your message input field does your recording icon show up.

3   Then tap on to send your message.

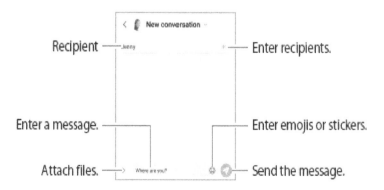

Recipient ——— Jenny

Enter recipients.

Enter a message. ———

Enter emojis or stickers.

Attach files. ——— Where are you?

Send the message.

View messages

1 Open your Messages app then tap on Conversations.

2 On your messages list, choose any contact or phone number.

- To respond to your message, touch your input field for messages, type your message, then tap on 🕖 .

- Pinch or spread your two fingertips apart on your screen to adjust your font size.

Sorting out your messages

Messages can be sort by category and effortlessly manageable.

Your messages can sort using category and you can manage them effortlessly

Open your Messages application, then select Conversations →then tap ✛ .

To enable your category option when it is not visible, tap on ⋮ select Settings and press on Conversation categories toggle.

Deleting messages

You must tap & hold any message before tapping Delete in order to delete it.

Change your message settings

Open your Messages app, then tap $\vdots \rightarrow$ then select Settings. You may block any unwanted messages, or even change your notification settings, & many more.

Internet

Use the Internet to look for information, & bookmark your favorite's websites to your favorites for easy access.

1   Open your Internet app.

2   Then enter any keyword or your web address, then tap on Go.

Drag your fingers down slightly on your screen to see your toolbars.

For quick switching between tabs swiftly, swipe to your left / right on your address field.

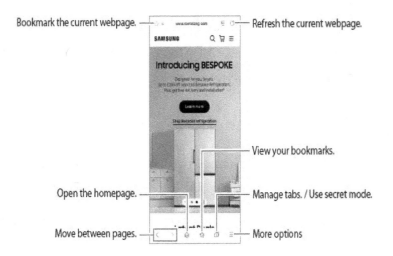

Bookmark the current webpage.
Refresh the current webpage.
View your bookmarks.
Open the homepage.
Manage tabs. / Use secret mode.
Move between pages.
More options

Employing the secret mode

You can stop other people from seeing your bookmarks, saved pages, search and browsing histories if you establish password for your secret mode.

1   Tap on 🔲 → Turn on Secrets mode.

2   Tap on your Lock Secrets mode toggle to enable it, then tap on Start, then setup your password for the secret mode.

The toolbars' color will change on your device when it is in secret mode. Tap on 🔲 → select Turn off Secrets mode to disable secret mode.

When on secret mode, one cannot use certain features, like your screen capture.

Multi window

Intro.

With the multi window, you may run two applications in split screen mode simultaneously. In your pop-up view, you may also run multiple applications simultaneously.

Some applications might not support feature.

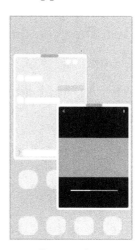

Split screen view   Pop-up view

Splitting your screen view

1   To view your list for recently used applications, tap on your Recents button.

2   To open any application on split screen's view, you should swipe left / right, then tap its icon, and then select Open in splits screen's view.

3   Choose a different app to open from your list of apps.

Launching applications from your Edge panel

1   Drag the Edge panel handle to the center of the screen while using an application.

2   Tap & hold down any app, then drag it toward your left, then you drop it when Drop here's to open shows up.

The chosen application will open in split screen mode.

You may set to open any application on your split screen's view when you tap it once. Then tap $\equiv$ → then select Edit → tap $\vdots$ then double tap beneath Opens in split screen views. when you tap on the Show recents apps toggle to enable it, you can open your recently used applications in your split screen views from your Edge panel.

Adding application pairs

To open frequently used applications in together with one tap in split screen view, add them to your Edge panel.

1   In your split screen view, tap on the circles that is between your app windows.

2   Then tap on ⊞.

The applications you use in your split screen's view are going to be saved in your Edge panel as an application pair.

Adjusting your window sizes

To change the size of your app windows, drag on the circles that's between them.

Whenever you drag on the circles between your application windows towards your screen edge, your window will get maximized.

Pop-up view

1   To open your list for recently used applications, tap your Recents button.

2   To open any application on pop-up view, swipe left / right, then tap its icon, and then select Open in pop-up view.

87

3	Your pop-up view will display your application screen.

Whenever you are using pop-up window, tapping your Home button will cause your window to minimize and show as an application icon. Tap your application icon to return to your pop-up window.

Launching your applications from Edge panel

1	Move your Edge panels handle to your screen's center.

2	Holding down on an app will allow you to drag it towards your left & drop where Drop here for pop-ups views displays.

The chosen application will open in your pop-up window.

Moving your pop-ups windows

A pop-up window can be moved to new location by tapping and dragging its toolbar.

Samsung's Pay

Introduction

To swiftly and securely make payments both online & offline, register cards with Samsung Pay.

- Depending on your region, your smartphone might need to be connected to a mobile network or Wi-Fi in order to use Samsung Pay for making payments.

- The availability of this feature may vary based on your model or service provider.

- Depending on your service provider / model, different steps may need to be taken for your initial setup & card registration.

Setup your Samsung Pay

Upon launching this application for the very firsts time or restarting it following data reset, adhere to your on-screen directions to finish your initial setting up.

1   Open your Samsung Pay application.

2   Sign into your Samsung's account then go through the terms & conditions as you read & agree.

3   Set up a PIN and your fingerprint for use while making payments. Such PIN shall be needed to verify a number of Samsung Pay operations, including paying bills and unlocking your app.

Registering cards

Open your Samsung Pay app then follow your on-screen directions to complete the registration of your card.

Making payments

1   You should tap & hold down a card image that on your bottom screen and then drag it up. You can also open your Samsung Pay application. Next, swipe left / right to choose a card for use from your card list.

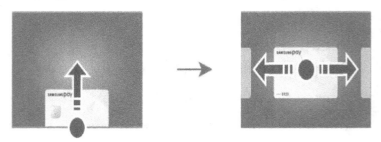

2.   Enter your PIN you set for payment or scan your fingerprint.

3.   Touch the backside of your mobile device to your card reader.

Your payment will be executed as soon as your card reader recognizes your card details.

- With respect to your network connections, payments could fail to be processed.
- Depending on your card readers, different payment verification method might be used.

Cancelling your payments
You may cancel your payments by going to the place you've made them.

To choose which cards you used, swipe right or left on your card list. To finish the payment cancellation process, adhere to your on-screen directions.

Samsung Notes

You can create notes by writing by hand, using a keyboard, or by drawing on your screen. Images and audio recordings can also be added to your notes.

Create notes

1 Open your Samsung Notes app, then tap on ⊡, then you create note.

You may change your input method via tapping ⊘ /

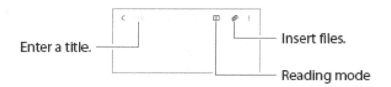

Enter a title. —— Insert files.

—— Reading mode

2 After writing your note, save it by tapping your Back button. To save your note in a different file format, tap on ⋮ → then select Saves as file.

Deleting notes

You should tap & hold down any note for deleting then tap on Delete.

Samsung Health

Introduction

You can better manage your fitness and well-being with Samsung Health. Establish goals for your fitness, monitor your development, and keep records of your general well-being and fitness. In addition, you may view health advice while comparing the number of steps in your records with those of other Samsung's Health users. For further details, go to www.samsung.com/samsung-health.

Employing the Samsung Health

Open the Samsung Health application. To finish the setup, follow the on-screen directions when using this app for the first time or when you resume it following a data reset. Select Manage items from your list of home cards at your bottom of your Samsung's Health home screens to make changes to any item.

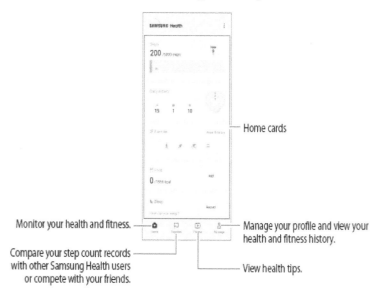

Monitor your health and fitness.

Home cards

Manage your profile and view your health and fitness history.

Compare your step count records with other Samsung Health users or compete with your friends.

View health tips.

- Certain features might not be accessible based on your location.

- Vibration may impact your step count when you use your steps card while taking a train or car ride.

93

Samsung Members

Samsung Members provide customers with support services like diagnosing device issues, allowing users to submit questions & error reports, sharing information with other members of the Galaxy user's community, and viewing the most recent news and advice. In addition, Samsung Members enable you to report errors & share information.

Samsung Members can assist you with any issues you may run into when using your device. They provide diagnostic services for device problems allow users to submit questions & error reports, and allow you to share information with other members of the Galaxy users' community or view the most recent news and tips.

Samsung Galaxy Global Goal

A sustainable society is one of the objectives of Global Goals, that was established by UN Generals Assembly in 2015. These goals offer the capacity to halt climate change, combat inequality, and eradicate poverty.

Discover more regarding the global goals & become involved in the drive for a much better future through Samsung Global's Goals.

Galaxy Shop

You can access your Samsung webpage to see various kinds of info related to products.

Open your Galaxy Shop application.

Galaxy Wearable

The Galaxy Wearable is an application that helps you in managing your wearable gadgets. You can personalize your wearable device's configuration and applications by connecting your device to it.

Open your app for your Galaxy Wearable.

Tap on Start for the connection of your device to your wearable. comply with the instructions given on your screen to finish your setup. For further details on connecting and using your wearable with your device, consult the user manual that comes with it.

Calendar

Achieve your schedule by inputting the upcoming events in your planner.

Creating events

1   Open your Calendar application then tap on ⊕ or you double-tap on a date.

When that date has saved task or events on it already, you should tap on that date, then tap ⊕.

2   Then enter the details of your event then tap Save.

Synchronizing events to your accounts

1   Open your Settings application, then tap on Accounts & backup → then select Manage accounts, then choose your account for syncing with.

2   Then Tap on Sync account & tap on the Calendar toggle for activating it.

Open your Calendar application and then tap → ~→ select Manage calendars →✚ to add up accounts for syncing with. Next, choose the account you want to synch with and log in. A blue circle appears next to your account's name when it is added.

In addition to the accounts to sync with, carefully open the Calendar application and then tap☰ →⚙ → Manage calendars →➕. Then, hand-picked an account to sync with and sign in. When the account has been added, you will experience a blue circle presented next to the account name.

Reminder

Set conditions for receiving notifications, and register your to-do items for reminders.

- Connect to a mobile or Wi-Fi network to get notifications that are more accurate.

- The GPS feature needs to be turned on in order to use your location reminders. The availability of location reminders varies based on your model.

Starting your Reminder

Open your Calendar app then tap on☰→ select Reminder. Your Reminder screen is going to display and your Reminder application icon (🔔) will get added into your Apps screen.

Creating your reminders

1   Open your Reminder application.

2   Then tap on $+$, enter your details, then tap on Save.

Completing your reminders

On your reminders list, you should tap on $\bigcirc$ or choose a reminder then tap Complete.

Restoring your reminders

You can restore reminders that have already been completed.

1   On your reminders list, select $\equiv \rightarrow$ then tap on Completed.

2   Choose any category then tap on Edit.

3   Select any reminder you want to restore, then tap on Restore.

Such reminders will get added into your reminders list then you will get reminded again.

Deleting your reminders

Choose a reminder and tap on Delete for deleting it.

To delete several reminders, hold down the reminder, then tick the ones you want to delete, then you tap on Delete.

My Files

You can access & manage a variety of files stored on your device.

Open your My Files application.

Tap on Analyze storage to scan for irrelevant data & free up your storage on your device. Press Q to search for folders or files.

Clock

This allows you Set time for an event, check the time in numerous cities worldwide, set an alarm, or pick a time period. Open your Clock application.

Calculator

You carry out simple or challenging computations. Open your Calculator application.

- ⊕ : View your calculation history. Press Clear history to erase your history. Press ⊞ to exit your calculation history's panel

- ⊞ : Apply your unit conversion utility. Many quantities, including area, length, and temperature, can be changed into different units.

- ⊞ : Make your scientific calculator display.

SmartThings

You can control & manage your smart appliances & Internets of Things (IoT) items using your smartphone.

To see further info, open the SmartThings application and then tap Menu → How to use.

1   Open your SmartThings application.

2   Then tap on Devices → then select Adds device or tap ✚.

3   Choose a device then connect to it using your on-screen directions.

- Depending on your shared contents or the type of devices connected, several connection methods may apply.

- Devices you could connect might vary based on your region. The features that are available may vary based on your device that is connected.

Samsung's warranty does not cover faults or defects pertaining to connected devices. When errors /

defects happen in connected devices, reach out to your device's manufacturer.

Smart View

Connect your mobile device to TV or monitor that supports screen mirroring so you may see your contents displayed in a larger screen.

1 Open your notification panel, then swipe down, then you tap on (Smart View).

2 Choose the device for mirroring the screen of your device.

Depending on your TV model, your resolution could vary when playing a video using Smart View.

Music Share

Introduction

You can share your speaker's Bluetooth connection with someone else if it's already connected to mobile device using your Music Share's feature. The same song can be played on both your own or someone's Galaxy Buds.

Only devices which supports Music Share function can use this feature.

Share your Bluetooth speaker

Using your Bluetooth's speaker, you can play music from both your mobile device and that of your friend's device.

1 Ensure that your Bluetooth speaker and smartphone have been connected.

2.To enable Music Sharing on your smartphone, open your Settings application, select Connections → then tap on Bluetooth → ⋮ then select Advanced, then touch your Music Share's switch.

Tap on Music Share to access more features, like deciding who can share your smartphone with you.

3. Choose your speaker in your list of Bluetooth devices in your friend's smartphone.

4. On your device, accept your connection's request. Your speaker is going to be shared.

Your music playing in your smartphone gets paused once you use your friend's smartphone to play music.

Using your Galaxy Buds to listen to songs with friends

Together, you and your friend can use your smartphone's buds to listen to songs on your phone.

The Buds series of Galaxy is the only devices to support this feature.

1 Ensure that every smartphone and set of earbuds are connected.

2   In the smartphone of your friend, Open your Settings application, then tap Connections → select Bluetooth → ⋮ → then select Advanced, then tap on your Music's Share switch for activating it.

3   Tap on Music Share to access more features, like deciding who can share the devices with you.

4   On your mobile device, open your notification panel then tap on Media output.

5   Choose your friend's Buds from your list of detected devices by tapping Music Share.

6   You should accept connections request in your friend's mobile.

You may listen to music on both Buds simultaneously while you play it on your smartphone.

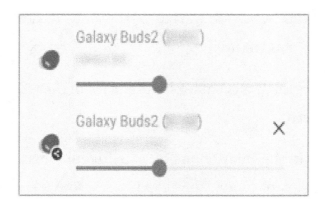

Linking to Windows

To immediately access the data of your device, including messages or photos, on a Windows PC, simply connect your mobile device to the computer.

You can use the computer to accept calls and messages when they enter.

- It is suggested to employ the most recent version of the Windows as well as the Your Phone app for completely using this feature.

- An account with Microsoft is needed for accessing this feature. You may log in to any Microsoft service or devices, including Windows 10 and Microsoft Office, by creating an account.

Connecting to computer

1 Open your Settings app then tap on Advanced features → then Links to Windows.

2 Follow your on-screen directions for completion of your connection.

Viewing data and notifications from your device on the computer Open your Phone application on your computer then choose a category that you want.

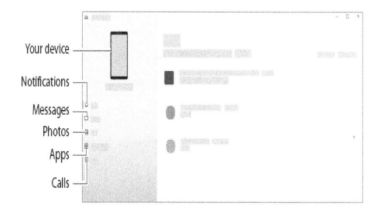

The features available and menus could differ depending on your model or software version.

Google applications

Google offers business, social media, and entertainment apps. Certain apps may demand a Google account in order to use them.

Go to the help menu of each app to discover additional information about it.

- Chrome: Use it for browsing websites and do information searches.

- Gmail: Use your Google's Mail service to send and receive emails.

- Maps: Use them to see where you are in relation to other locations, search the globe map, and find your current location.

- YT Music: Take in a variety of tunes and videos from YouTube Music. You may also listen to and explore the collections of music that are saved on your smartphone.

- Google Plays Movies and TV: Get movies & TV shows on the Play Store or rent them.

- Drive: Share and save your content in your cloud, accessible from any location.

- YouTube: Watch as well as create videos & share these with others.

- Photos: Find, organize, and edit every photo and video you have from different sources at one location.

- Google: Use your device or the Internet to swiftly search for contents.

- Duo: Have a basic video call.

- Messages: Use your computer or smartphone to send & receive messages as well as share different types of content, including photos and videos.

Certain applications might be unavailable depending on your model or service provider.

Chapter 7
Gallery

Introduction

The Gallery allows you view your photos and videos that are saved on your smartphone. Additionally, you can make stories and organize photos and videos via album.

Using your Gallery

Open your Gallery application.

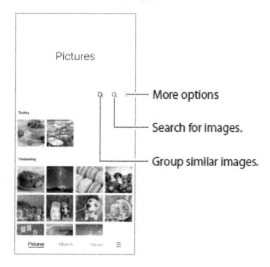

Grouping identical images

Open your Gallery app then tap⊡for grouping similar photos and displaying only your best captured shots as preview of your photos. You can view every image in your group by tapping on your image preview.

Viewing images

Open your Gallery application and choose a picture.

Slide left / right on your screen for access to different files.

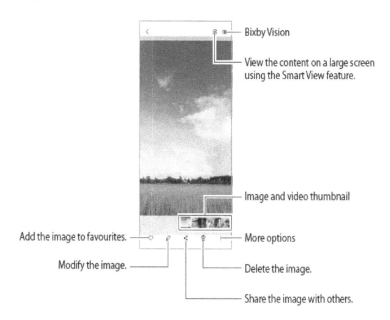

Bixby Vision

View the content on a large screen using the Smart View feature.

Image and video thumbnail

Add the image to favourites.

Modify the image.

More options

Delete the image.

Share the image with others.

Cropping enlarged photos

1 Open your Gallery application then choose any image.

2 Spread your two fingers apart on that spot that you want it to save then tap ⊙ .

The cropped place will automatically be saved as a file.

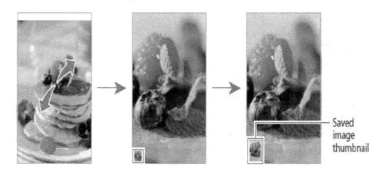

Saved
image
thumbnail

Viewing videos

Open your Gallery application and choose any video for playing. To view other files, swipe to your right or left side on your screen.

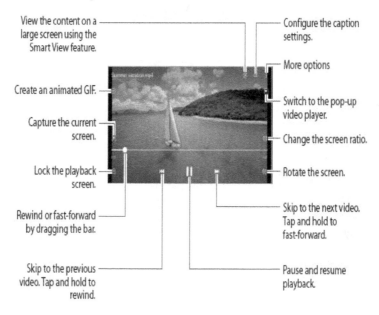

View the content on a large screen using the Smart View feature.

Configure the caption settings.

More options

Create an animated GIF.

Capture the current screen.

Switch to the pop-up video player.

Change the screen ratio.

Lock the playback screen.

Rotate the screen.

Rewind or fast-forward by dragging the bar.

Skip to the next video. Tap and hold to fast-forward.

Skip to the previous video. Tap and hold to rewind.

Pause and resume playback.

If you want to modify your brightness or volume of the playback, drag your finger upward or downward on your left / right side of your screen, respectively.

Swipe to your right or left on your playback screen to fast-forward or rewind.

Albums

You can create albums then sort out your photos and videos.

1   Open your Gallery app then tap on Albums →

⋮ → select Create album for creating an album.

2   Choose your album, tap on Add items, then copy/move your pictures or videos that you want.

Stories

Whenever you save or capture pictures and videos, your device will process their date & location tags, organize your pictures and videos, then it creates stories.

Open your Gallery app, then tap on Stories after which select any Story.

To add / delete photos or videos, choose a story then tap on ⋮ → Adds or Edit.

Syncing your photos and videos

Open your Gallery application, then tap on ≡ →
select Settings → then tap Sync with OneDrive, then
follow your on-screen directions for the completion of
your sync. There will be cloud syncing with your
Gallery application. Your captured images and videos
will be cloud-stored once your Gallery application is
cloud-synced. Using your Gallery application and
other devices, you may view videos and images that
have been stored on the cloud.

You can select Microsoft OneDrive as your cloud
storage option after you connect your Samsung's and
Microsoft accounts.

Deleting photos / videos

Open your Gallery app, then tap & hold down any
picture or video, or any story for deletion, then you tap
on Delete.

Using your recycle bin function

You may retain your deleted videos and pictures in
your recycle bin. After a specific amount of time, your
files will get deleted.

Open your Gallery app, then tap on ☰→ select Settings, then tap on Recycle bin toggle for activating it.

To view your files in your recycle bin, open your Gallery application then tap on ☰→ Recycle bin.

AR Zone

Introduction

You can access AR-related features at AR Zone. Select any feature & capture amusing images or videos.

Launching your AR Zone

You can use these below methods for launching AR Zone:

- Open your AR Zone application.

- Open your Camera app then tap on MORE → select AR ZONE.

Certain features might not be accessible based on your model or service provider.

AR Emojis Studio

You can create emojis however you want it, and make it fun when using them with different features.

Creating AR Emoji

1   Open your AR Zone app then tap on AR Emoji Studios.

2   You may select a ready-made emoji for getting started quickly. Choose an emoji by swiping left/right, then tap on ⊙.

To create your own emoji, either choose an image or snap a selfie.

3   To make an emoji, adhere to your on-screen directions.

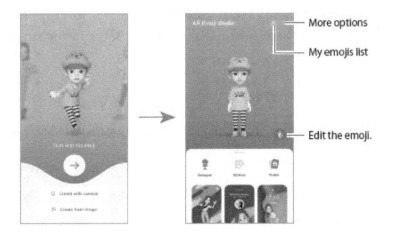

Selecting AR emoji for use

Open your AR Zone application, then tap on AR Emoji Studios →⌂, then you select any emoji you desire.

114

Delete AR emojis

Open your AR Zone application, tap on AR Emoji Studios→ 👤→🗑, tick the emojis for delete, then tap on Delete.

Create AR emoji's short clip & decorate device using it

Your emojis can be used to produce a short clip that you can use as your call background picture or wallpaper.

1   Open your AR Zone application then tap on AR Emoji Studios.

2   Choose Create video, Lock screen or Call screen.

3   Then select any template you like.

To change your background image, you should tap on 🖼.

4   Tap on Save to save your video.

You may view your saved videos from your Gallery.

5   To use your video directly, you should select an option on your bottom screen.

Create contact profile using AR emoji

1   Make use of any emoji for your Contacts application and Samsung account profile picture.

2   Open your AR Zone application, then select AR Emoji Studios.

3   Tap Profile, then choose an emoji.

4   Choose a desired stance.

5   Press on Done → then Save.

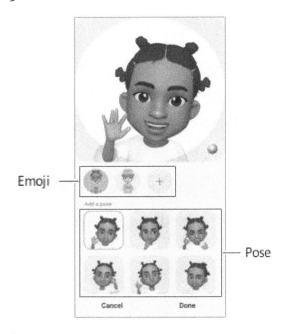

AR Sticker Emojis

Make your own stickers by combining the expressions & actions of your emojis. Your emojis stickers can be used on social media platforms or in message correspondence.

Create your stickers

1 Open your AR Zone app then tap on AR Emojis Stickers.

2 Then tap on ┬ on top of your stickers list.

3 Edit your stickers however you like then tap on Save.

You may view your stickers that you've created via tapping on Custom.

Delete AR stickers emoji

Open your AR Zone application then tap on AR Emojis Stickers → ⋮ → then select Delete stickers. Choose your emoji stickers for deletion then tap Delete.

Using your AR emoji stickers in chats

You may employ your emojis stickers in text messages or on social media to participate in conversations. The subsequent actions are a demonstration of how to employ your emoji stickers on your Messages app.

117

1   As you are composing message in your Messages application, tap on ☺ on your Samsung keyboard.

2   Tap on your emoji icon.

3   Choose one of the emoji stickers.

That emoji sticker gets inserted.

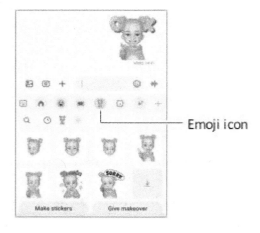

Emoji icon

AR Doodle

Make amusing videos by recording doodles or handwriting on faces or other surfaces. When a face / space is recognized by your camera, that doodles on such face will move with the face, while doodles on the space remain fixed in place regardless of camera movement.

1   Open your AR Zone application tap on AR Doodle.

When your camera recognizes your subject, your recognition area will display on your screen.

2   Tap on 🖊️ & write/draw on your recognition area.

- You may also write / draw outside of the recognition area when you've switch to your rear camera.

- If you tap on ⊙ and begin to doodle and you can also record yourself doodling.

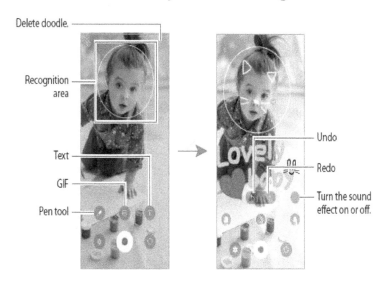

3   Tap on ⦿ to record your video.

4 Tap ▣ on stop recording your video.

Your video can be viewed & shared in your Gallery.

Depending on the camera being used, your preview screen's features could vary.

Radio

Open your Radio application

An earphone must be plugged in before using the FM app, as it acts as a radio antenna.

When your FM radio is turned on for the very first time, it automatically searches for and remembers available stations.

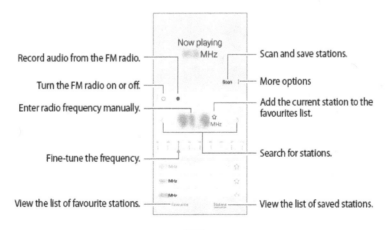

Playing through your speaker

Rather than using your connected headphone, you can use the speaker to listen to your radio.

Press ⋮→ tap play through speaker.

Game Launcher

With Game Launcher, all of the games you've downloaded from your Play Store & Galaxy Store are conveniently collected in one location. For easier gaming, you may set your smartphone in game mode.

Open your Game Launcher application and choose your preferred game.

- In case your Game Launcher is not visible, open your Settings application, select Advanced features, then press your Game Launcher toggle to make it operational.

- Your Game's Launcher screen will automatically display games that have been downloaded from your Play Store & Galaxy Store. To view your games, tap on My games →⋮→ then select Add games.

Removing game from your Game Launcher

You should Tap on My games, then hold down any game, then you tap on Remove.

Changing your performance mode

The performance mode of your game can be changed. Open your Game Launcher application, then tap on ☰ → then select Game Booster → then tap Game optimization, then you select your mode.

- Performance: The goal here is to provide you with the best gaming performance possible.

- Standard: This strikes a balance between battery consumption duration and performance.

- Battery saver: When playing games, this preserves battery life.

Your battery power performance could differ by game.

Transfer data in former device (via Smart Switch)

You can employ Smart Switch for transferring data from your former smartphone into your new smartphone. Open your Settings app then tap on Accounts & backup → select Brings data from old devices.

- This feature might not be supported in certain devices as well as computers.
- Limitations apply. Check out www.samsung.com/smartswitch more info. Copyright is a crucial matter for Samsung. Transfer only content which you have or are authorized to transfer

Wirelessly transfer data

Use Wi-Fi Direct to wirelessly transfer data to your device from your old device.

1   On your previous device, Open your Smart Switch.

When you don't have the application yet, download it on the Play Store/Galaxy Store.

2. Open your Settings application in your device, then tap on Accounts & backup → select Brings data from old devices.

3.Place your devices close to each other.

4 On your former device, tap on Send data → then select Wireless.

5 From your device, choose the operating system from your former device, then tap on Receive data, then tap on Wireless.

6 Press Allow on your former device.

7 To transfer your data, choose any option on your smartphone, tap Next, then adhere to your on-screen directions.

Backing up & restoring data with your external storage

You can use your external storage to transfer data, like the microSD card.

1 Make a backup copy of your old device's data to an external storage.

2 Insert your external storage devices into your device or connect it to it.

3 Open your Settings app on your device, then select Accounts & backup → then select External storage's transfer.

4. Below the "Restores from SD cards" menu, choose your backup date.

5. For transferring data, choose an option, tap on Next, then adhere to your on-screen directions.

Transferring your backed-up data from computer

Transfer data among your device and a PC. The Smart Switch PC version application can be downloaded at www.samsung.com/smartswitch. Backup your data from that of your old smartphone to a computer, then sync it to your device.

1 On your computer, check out www.samsung.com/smartswitch to download your Smart Switch.

2 On your computer, open Smart Switch.

 when your former device wasn't a Samsung device, your backup data to a computer employing a program given by your device's manufacturer. Next, move on to the fifth action.

3. Use the USB cord that came with the former device to connect it to your computer.

4. To backup data from your device, use your computer's on-screen instructions.

After that, unplug your former device off your computer.

5. Use your USB cord to connect your mobile device to your computer.

6. For transferring data to your device, follow your on-screen steps on your computer.

Settings

The Samsung accounts

To manage your Samsung's account, log in. Select Samsung account from your Settings screen.

Connections

Options

To change your settings for different connections, including Bluetooth and Wi-Fi.

On your Settings screen, you should tap on Connections.

- Wi-Fi: Turn on your Wi-Fi feature for connecting to a network and gain access to other network devices or the Internet. For additional information, see Wi-Fi.

- Bluetooth: To share media files or data among Bluetooth-enabled devices, use Bluetooth.

Transform settings for different connections, likely as the Wi-Fi feature and the Bluetooth.

On the Settings screen, tap Connections.

- NFC & contactless payments: Configure your device so that it can scan near-field communication, or NFC, tags—which have product information on them. You may additionally employ this feature for payments and purchasing tickets for transport or events shortly after downloading your required applications. For further details, see NFC & contactless payments (models that support NFC).

- Flight mode: Configure your device to turn off all wireless connection's features. Only non-network services are available to you.

Follow the guidelines issued by your airline plus the instructions given by flight staff. When using your device, make sure it's in-flight mode at all times.

- Mobile networks: Set up the settings for your mobile network.

- Data usage: Track how much data you use and adjust your limitation's settings. Once you've consumed all of your allotted mobile data, configure your device to turn off your connection automatically.

Your data saver function can be used to stop some background-running applications from sending / receiving data. For more details, see Data saver.

You can additionally configure applications to always use your mobile data regardless of whether your device connects to a Wi-Fi connection.

- SIM cards manager: Adjust your SIM card settings and activate the SIM / USIM cards. See SIM card management for further details.

- Mobile Hotspot & Tethering: To share your device's mobile data connectivity to other devices, use it as mobile hotspot. See Mobile Hotspot for additional details about the hotspot.

When utilizing this feature, you can be charged extra.

- More connections settings: You can personalize settings for controlling other features.

Wi-Fi

For connection to a Wi-Fi connection and the access to the Internet or different network devices, turn on your Wi-Fi feature.

Connecting to Wi-Fi network

1 On your Settings screen, you should tap on Connections → select Wi-Fi then tap on your switch to enable it.

2 Choose any network from your Wi-Fi networks list.

Please take note that networks with a lock icon will request for a password.

- Without a password, your device will automatically reconnect to any Wi-Fi network once it has established a connection. To stop your device from automatically establishing a connection to the network, tap on the Auto reconnect toggle to disable it.

- Try restarting your wireless router or your Wi-Fi feature on your device if you are having trouble connecting to a network.

Viewing the quality of your Wi-Fi network information

View your quality information on your speed & stability of your Wi-Fi network.

On your Settings screen, you should tap on Connections → then select Wi-Fi & tap on the switch to enable it. Your Wi-Fi networks will have your network quality info shown beneath them. In case it is not visible, tap on ⋮ → Advanced then select Show network's quality info option to turn it on.

The Wi-Fi network quality info can be view, likely as the speed and stability.

Depending on your Wi-Fi network, your quality information might not display.

Sharing your passwords for Wi-Fi network

You may connect to a secured Wi-Fi connection without inputting your password if you ask someone who is already connected to share the network's password with you. This feature can only be used between devices that are in contact with one another, and the other device's screen must be switched on.

1 On your Settings screen, you should tap on Connections → then select Wi-Fi then tap on the switch to enable it.

2 Choose any network from the list of your Wi-Fi networks.

3 Then tap on Request password.

4 Accept your share request from your other device.

Your Wi-Fi password's is entered in your mobile device & it gets connected to your network

Wi-Fi Direct

The Wi-Fi Direct removes the need for an access point by connecting devices to Wi-Fi networks directly.

1   On your Settings screen, you should tap on Connections → then select Wi-Fi then tap on the switch for activating it.

2   Then tap on   → then select Wi-Fi Direct. Your detected devices will be listed.

When the device that you wish to connect with is absent from the list, demand that such device should turns on the Wi-Fi Direct feature.

3. To connect with a device, choose one.

Once the other devices approve Wi-Fi Direct connectivity request, your devices get connected.

Choose which device to disconnect in your list in order to disengage the connection.

Bluetooth

Use Bluetooth for sharing media files or data to other Bluetooth-capable devices.

- Samsung will not take responsibility for the loss, misuse or interception of the data received or sent through Bluetooth.

- Always make sure the devices you send and receive data from are reliable and adequately secured. The operational distance could be shortened when there are obstructions between both devices.

- It's possible that some devices won't work with yours, particularly those that haven't been tested or authorized by Bluetooth SIG.

132

- Avoid using your Bluetooth feature for illegal activities, such as file piracy or intercepting conversations without authorization for profit. The consequences of using the Bluetooth feature illegally are not Samsung's responsibility.

Pairing to other Bluetooth gadgets

1 On your Settings screen, select Connections → then select Bluetooth then tap on the switch for activating it. These detected devices are going to be listed.

2 Choose ant device for pairing.

when the device that you wish to pair to doesn't appear on your list, set that device to go into Bluetooth pairing modes. Consult the user manuals for that other device.

Your device will be visible for other devices all while your Bluetooth settings screens stays open.

3 You should accept Bluetooth connection request in your device for confirmation.

Whenever any other device confirms your Bluetooth connection request, both devices will be connected together.

To unpair your devices, you should tap on   next to your device name for unpair then tap on Unpair.

Sending & receiving data

The Bluetooth data transfer is supported by many applications. Contacts and media files are among the data that can be shared among other devices Bluetooth. Here are some examples of how to send a photograph to a different device.

1   Open your Gallery application then choose an image.

2   Then Tap on ⋖→ then select Bluetooth and choose a device for transferring your images to.

When the device that you desire to pair to does not appear in your list, demand that such device turn-on the visibility option.

3 You should accept Bluetooth connection demand from that other device.

(The NFC-enabled models) NFC & contactless payments

NFC (Near fields communication) tags with product information can be read with our device. You may additionally employ this feature for payments and purchasing of tickets use for events or transportation after downloading your needed applications.

There is an NFC antenna integrated within your device itself. Take care when handling the smartphone to prevent harm to your NFC antenna.

Read information in NFC tags

You can use your NFC feature to read product information from NFC tags.

1 On your Settings screen, should tap Connections then tap on NFC & contactless payments switch for activation.

2 Place your NFC antenna area on your device back close to an NFC tag. Information from your tag will display.

Make sure that your device's screen has been turned on & is unlocked. If not, your device won't be able to scan NFC tags or get data.

Making payments using your NFC feature

You have to sign up for mobile payment services before you can utilize your NFC feature for making payments. Get in touch with your service provider to register or find out more about the service.

1   On your Settings screen, you should tap on Connections then tap NFC & contactless payments toggle for activation.

2   Touch your NFC antenna space at your device back to your NFC card's reader.

3   Open your Settings screen, select Connections → then tap NFC & contactless payments → select Contactless payments → then tap on Payment, then

choose an app to set as your default payment application.

Not every payment app that is offered may be on your list of payment services.

Printing

Set up your printer's plug-ins that are installed on your device. Wi-Fi / Wi-Fi Direct connections to printers allow you to print documents or photos from your device.

It's possible that some printers won't work with your device.

Adding up printers' plug-ins

For the printers you wish to use your device with, add your printer plug-ins.

1   On your Settings screen, you should tap on Connections → then tap More connections settings → then select Printing → tap on Download plugin.

2 Choose the printer plug-in & install it.

3 Choose your installed plug-in.

When it comes to printers, your device automatically looks for ones which are connected to the exact same wireless network as it.

4 then select any printer you want to add.

For manually adding printers, tap on $\vdots$ → select Add printer.

Printing your contents

While viewing your content, like pictures or documents, then access your options list, then tap on Print → then Select a printer → then select All printers..., then pick a printer.

Printing methods could vary based on the type of content.

Sounds & vibration

Options

You can change settings of the different sounds on your device.

Select Sounds & vibration from your Settings screen.

- Sound mode: Select between silence, vibration, or sound modes for your device.

- Vibrates while ringing: configure your device for vibration & plays a ringtone over incoming calls.

- Temporary mute: Designate a time for your device to operate in silent mode.
- Ringtone: Modify your phone's call ringtone.
- Notifications sounds: Modify the sound used for notifications.
- System sound: Customize the sound for specific operations, such charging a device.
- Volume: Helps adjust the volume on your device.
- Call vibrations patterns: Allows you change your call pattern of vibration.
- Notifications vibrations pattern: Modify your vibration pattern for notifications.
- Vibration intensity: Change the force for your vibration notification.
- Systems sound/vibration control: Configure your device to vibrate or make sound in response to certain actions, including using the touchscreen.
- Sound quality & effects: Adjust your sound quality & effects on your device.

- Separate apps sound: Configure your device to independently play media sound in the different audio device from a certain app.

Certain features might be unavailable based on your model.

Sound quality & effects

Adjust your sound quality & effects on your device.

Tap on Sounds & vibration → then select Sound quality & effects from your Settings screen.

- Dolby Atmos: Choose a surround sounds mode optimized for multiple forms of audio, like in movies, songs, and voice. You can enjoy flowing, moving audio's sounds all around you when you use Dolby Atmos.

- Dolby Atmos as for gaming: While playing games, enjoy your Dolby Atmos sounds optimized for gaming.

- Equalizer: To experience optimal sound, choose an option specialized to a certain kind of music.

- Adapt sounds: Setups the ideal sound you need.

Using certain features may require connecting an earphone, depending on your model.

Separate application sounds

You can configure the mobile device to play audio from a certain application on a connected headphone or Bluetooth speaker.

For instance, you can use your Bluetooth speaker in your car to hear what's playing from your Music app while using your device's speakers to listen to your Navigation app.

1   On your Settings screen, you should tap on Sounds & vibration → then Separate apps sound and tap the switch to activate it.

2   Choose any application to play your media sounds from separately then tap your Back button.

3   Then you select any device to play your selected application's media sound.

Wallpapers & styles

Modify your locked screen's and your home screen's wallpaper. Tap on Wallpaper & style from your Settings screen.

Themes

Change your Home screen, icon, & locked screen visuals on your smartphone by applying different themes.

On your Settings screen, you should tap on Themes.

Home screen

Set up your Home screen's configuration, including your screen layout. Select the Home screen from your Settings screen.

Lock screen

Options

You can change your settings of your locked screen.

From your Settings screen, you should tap on Lock screen.

- Screens lock types: This changes the methods of your screen lock.

- Smart Lock: Configure your device to be unlocked automatically upon detection of trusted locations / devices.

- Secured lock settings: Adjust your screen lock configuration for your chosen lock method.

- Always On Displays: Configure your device to show information even when your screen is off.
- Wallpaper services: Configure your device to make use of wallpaper features like Dynamic Lock screens.
- Clock style: Modify your locked screen's clock's color and type.
- Roaming clock: When roaming, set your clock to display your home or local time zones in your locked screen.
- Widgets: Modify the properties of the objects visible on your screen that is locked.
- Contact information: Configure your device to display contact details, including email address, in your locked screen.
- Notifications: Configure your locked screen to display notifications.
- Shortcuts: On your locked screen, choose which applications to display shortcuts to.
- About Lock screens: View your legal information and your Lock screen versions.

- Depending on your model or service provider, some features might be unavailable.

The options that are available may vary based on the method of your screen lock used.

Smart Lock

You can configure your device to automatically unlock and stay unlocked when trusted places or devices are discovered.

When you arrive home, for instance, if you have designated your house to be a trusted location, your device will recognize your location and unlock itself.

On your Settings screen, you should tap on Lock screen → then select Smart Lock then you follow your on-screen directions to complete your setup.

- Available only once you've selected a method of screen lock, you can use this feature.

- If you refrain from using your device over four hours or once you turn it on, you must use your PIN, password or pattern that you've selected to unlock your screen.

You can unlock your phone screen by using the pattern, PIN, or password you have set.

Chapter 8
Biometrics & security

Options

You can change your settings use for securing your device.

On your device Settings screen, you should tap on Biometrics & security.

- Face recognition: The face recognition helps you to Set your device for unlocking your screen, through the use of your face.

- Fingerprints: Helps you register fingerprints for unlocking your screen.

- More biometrics settings: This lets you change your settings for your biometric data. Addition you may check out the version for your biometrics securities patch & to search for updates.

- Google's Play Protect: Allow you setup your device to check for harmful apps and behavior and warn about potential harm and remove them.

- Security update: This lets you Check latest updates & view your software version on your device.

- Google Plays system updates: Helps you check latest updates & view your Google Plays system versions.

- Finds My Mobile: You can switch on or off this feature. Visit the Samsung's Finds My Mobile webpage at findmymobile.samsung.com to monitor and manage your stolen or missing device.

- Samsung's Pass: Use your biometric information to quickly and securely confirm your identity. See Samsung's Pass for additional details.

- Secure Folder: To keep your apps and confidential content safe from prying eyes, this helps build a secured folder.

- Private Share: Use blockchain technology to safely share your files to others.

- Install unknown applications: Configure your device to permit installation from unknown application sources.

- Encrypts/decrypt SD card: This set your device for encryption of files in any memory card.

Your device won't be capable of reading your files that are encrypted once you reset it to its factory settings while keeping this setting option enabled. Before you reset your device, disable this setting.

- Others security settings: You can configure more security settings.

certain features might be unavailable all depending on your model or service provider.

Secure Folder

Your sensitive applications and content, including contacts and pictures, are protected from unwanted access with Secure Folder. Your private apps and content are safe even when your smartphone is unlocked.

Secure Folder acts as a distinct secured area for storage. It is not possible to share data from a Secure Folder with other devices via unauthorized means like

USB / Wi-Fi Direct. Any attempt to modify software or alter your operating system will result in Secure Folder becoming automatically locked & unusable. Ensure that you back up the copy of your data to a secure location before storing it in a secure folder.

Setting up your Secure Folder

1 Open your Settings app & tap on Biometrics & security → then select Secure Folder.

2 Then you follow your on-screen direction to complete your setup.

The screen of your secure Folder is going to appear, then your Secure Folder application icon ( ) will then be added to your Apps screen.

For changing the icon or name of your Secure Folder, you should tap on ⋮ → then select Customize.

- When you open your Secure Folder application, with your preset lock style.

- You can use your account on Samsung to reset your Secured Folder unlocking code if you lose it. To unlock your locked screen, you should tap on your bottom button and enter your password for your Samsung account.

Configuring auto locking condition for your Secure Folder

1   Open your Secure Folder application & tap on ⋮ → then select Settings → then tap on Auto locks Secured Folder.

2   You should then choose any option.

For manually locking your Secured Folder, you should tap on ⋮ → then select Lock & exit.

Moving your content into Secure Folder

You can move content, like videos and pictures, to Secure Folder. To move a picture from your default storage into the Secure Folder, use the following steps.

1   Open your Secure Folder application and tap ⋮ → then select Add files.

2   Then you tap Images, then tick your images for moving, then you tap Done.

3   Then tap on Move.

Your chosen items will then be transferred to the Secure Folder and removed from your original folder. For copying items, select Copy.

Depending on your type of content, different methods may be used for moving it.

Moving the content from your Secure Folder

You can Move contents from your Secure Folder into the appropriate app's default storage. An instance of moving a photo from your Secure Folder into your default storage is shown in the following steps.

1   Open your Secure Folder application then you tap on the Gallery.

2   Pick any image & tap ⋮ → then select Moves out of Secured Folder.

Your selected items are going to move into the Gallery in your default storage.

Adding up applications

You can add any application to use on your Secure Folder.

1   Open your Secure Folder application then you tap ✚.

2   After which tick one / many installed apps on your device and then you tap Add.

Removing of apps from your Secure Folder

To remove an app, press and hold it, then select Uninstall.

Adding up your accounts

You should add your Google, Samsung, and other accounts. To get your accounts to sync to your applications in your Secure Folder.

1   Open your Secure Folder application then tap on ⋮ → select Settings → tap on Manage accounts → then you select Add account.

2   Choose any account service.

3   Then you follow your on-screen directions for completing your account setup.

Hiding your Secure Folder

You may hide your Secure Folder's shortcut from your Apps screen.

Open your Secure Folder application, tap ⋮ → then you select Settings, then, to disable it, press the Adds Secured Folder to Apps screens switch.

Alternatively, to disable the feature, open your notification panel, slide down, then you touch ⊙ (Secure Folder). When ⊙ (Secure Folder) is not shown on your quick panel, then tap on ⊙ and drag on the button to add it.

To restore your Secure Folder's visibility, open your Settings application, select Biometrics & security → then you tap on Secure Folder, then you activate it by tapping the Adds Secure Folders to Apps screens switch.

On the other hand, launch the notification panel, kindly swipe downwards, and then hand-pick ⊙ (Secure Folder) to disable the feature. If you are unable to find 🔘 (Secure Folder) on the quick panel,

tap ⚪ and drag the button over to add it.

If you want to show the Secure Folder again, launch the Settings app, tap Biometrics and security → Secure Folder, and then tap the Add Secure Folder to Apps screen switch to activate it.

Uninstalling your Secure Folder

You are able uninstalling your Secure Folder together with its contents and applications.

Open your Secure Folder application and select ⋮ → then tap settings → then select more settings → then tap on uninstall.

To create a backup copy of your content prior to uninstalling your Secure Folder. You should tick on Move media's files out of Secure Folder then select Uninstall. To view your data that has been backed up from your Secure Folder, open My Files app's, select the internal storage → then you select Download → then tap on Secure Folder.

Notes saved on a Samsung device note won't Backed up.

Privacy

You can modify your settings for your privacy.

On your device screen, tap on Privacy.

- Permissions used in last 24 hours: This allows you to view your feature's permission or app usage history.

- Permission manager: Helps you to view your list of the features & apps which has the that permission for using them. Your permission settings, can also be edited.

- Controls & alerts: This helps you setup the settings to access your apps.

- Samsung: This allows you to manage your personal data which are connected to the account of your Samsung and modify your Customization Service settings.

- Google: This configures your advanced settings of your privacy.

Certain features might not be accessible based on your model or service provider.

Location

You can change your settings for the permission location information.

In your Settings screen, you should tap on Location.

- App permission: This helps you view your list of applications which have permission for accessing your device's location, then edit your permission settings.

- Location services: Check out the location-related services your device is currently using.

- Current access: You can view which applications require your recent location info.

Digital Wellbeing & parental controls

Check previous usage history of your smartphone and make advantage of the features to keep it from creeping over your life. You may also supervise your kids' internet usage and setup parental controls over them.

On your Settings screen, you should tap on the Digital Wellbeing & parental control.

- Screen time: Establish daily usage targets for your smartphone.

- App timers: Set a timer to restrict how much time you spend on each app each day. The software will become inactive and unavailable for usage after you surpass the limit.

- Focus mode: Turn on focus mode to keep your attention on your goals and block off distractions on your device. The apps that you gave permission to use can be employed while you are in focus mode.

- Bedtime mode: Turn on this feature to lessen eye strain just before bed and avoid having your sleep interrupted.

- Volume monitor: To safeguard your hearing, turn on your volume monitor.

- Driving monitor: Turn on your driving monitor for keeping track of how long you spend using your device behind the wheel.

- Parental controls: Supervise your kids' digital usage.

Battery & device care

Introduction

A review of your device battery life, storage capacity, memory, & system security of your device is given via device care feature. With a simple finger tap, you can additionally automatically optimize your device.

Optimize your device

In your Settings screen, select Battery & device care → then tap Optimize now.

The following activities are taken by the quick optimization feature to enhance device performance:

- Closing of applications running on your background.
- Managing of abnormal battery use.
- Scanning for your crashed applications & malware.

Employing the auto-optimization function

Whenever your device isn't being use, you have the option to set it to optimize automatically. Tap on → then select Automation → tap Auto optimizes daily then you tap on the switch for activating it. To configure your time for auto optimization, tap on the Time.

Battery

Verify the battery's remaining power and the device's time for use. For the devices using lower battery levels, you can conserve your battery power through activating power your saving features. From your Settings screen select Battery & device care → the select Battery.

- Power saving: To increase the battery's usage duration, turn on your power savings mode.

- Backgrounds usage limits: Set battery usage limits for infrequently used apps.

- More battery's settings: Set up your battery's advanced settings

Your usage time remaining indicates how long the battery will last before running out. Based on your device's operational conditions and settings, your remaining usage time could vary.

- Some applications that employ power-savings mode might not notify you. Power saving: You can enable the power saving mode to prolong the battery's usage time.

Storage

Verify the status of memory that is being used and available.

from your Settings screen, select Battery & device care → then tap on Storage. Choose a category and uninstall applications or delete files that you no longer need. Next, select or press and item, then you tap Delete / Uninstall.

Always monitor the status of the used and available memory.

- Your operating system & default applications take up space in your internal memory, therefore the real available capacity is less than the stated capacity.

If you upgrade your device, your available capacity might not remain the same.

- On your Samsung website, under Specifications section, you can see your internal memory's available capacity.

Memory

On your Settings screen, select the Battery & device care → then tap Memory.

To stop background app usage and speed up smartphone. tick each application on your list and then select Clean now.

Device protection

You can check your security status of your device. This feature helps you scan for malware on your device.

From your Settings screen, select Battery & device care → then select Device protection → tap on Scan phone.

The About phone

Get information on your device.

Select About phone from your Settings screen.

Tap Edit to change the name of your device.

- Status information: Access a range of device details, including your serial number, WiFi MAC addresses, & SIM card's status.

- Legal information: Access legal information regarding your device, including your open-source license and safety data.

- Software information: Access your device's software details, including the firmware and operating system versions.

- Battery info: Check your status & information of your device's battery. Access your device's information.